Sawan

MY BIG BOOK OF COLOURING

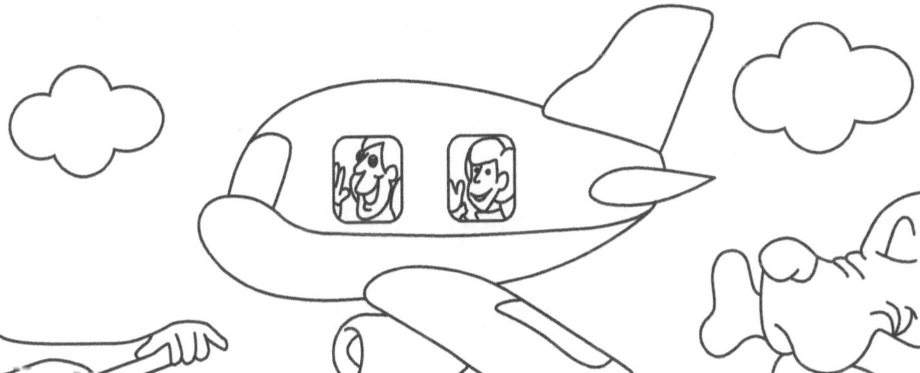

3

AF518496

MANOJ PUBLICATIONS
Delhi-110084 (INDIA)

PREFACE

Children have a natural curiosity for colours. It is the reason that their toys sport so many colours. Right from the age of 2-3, children start colouring different objects. Sometimes they show their skill on the walls, floors and doors too. Children start with chalks and crayons initially. Keeping children's love for colours in mind we have specially designed this book to develop their power of colourful imagination. But, be careful when children work with chalks and crayons. May be, because they try to bite them out of some natural instinct or tendency.

-Publishers

Edition : 2007

Price : Rs. 40/-

ISBN 978-81-310-0586-6

Printed by :
Jai Maya Offset

Manoj Publications
761, Main Road, Burari, Delhi-110084
Phones : 91-11-27611116, 27611349, **Fax** : 27611546 (**M**) 9868112194
E-mail : info@manojpublications.com, **Website**: www.manojpublications.com

Showroom:
1583-84, Dariba Kalan, Chandni Chowk, Delhi-110006
Phones : 91-11-23262174, 23268216 (**M**) 9818753569

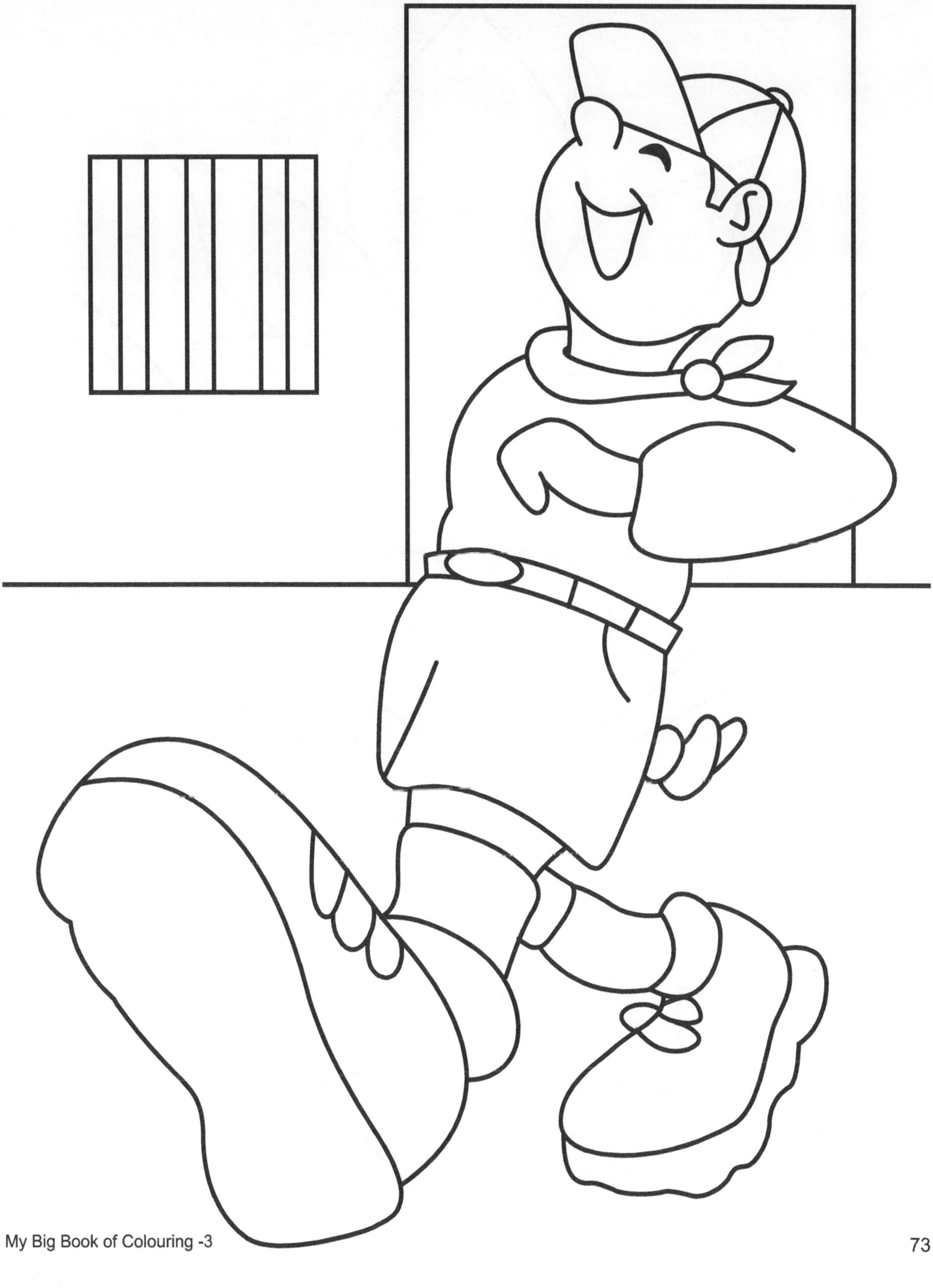